Spectacular Spots
Magníficas manchas

Written and Illustrated by / Escrito e Ilustrado por

Susan Stockdale

Translation by / Traducción de

Cristina de la Torre

in collaboration with the author / en colaboración con el autor

PEACHTREE
ATLANTA

For Todd, always
Para Todd, por siempre

Published by
PEACHTREE PUBLISHERS
1700 Chattahoochee Avenue
Atlanta, Georgia 30318-2112
www.peachtree-online.com

Text and illustrations © 2015 by Susan Stockdale
Spanish translation © 2017 by Peachtree Publishers

First bilingual trade paperback edition published in 2017.
Also available in an English-language hardcover edition: ISBN 978-1-56145-817-2.

Editor: Kathy Landwehr
Art direction by Loraine Joyner
Typesetting by Melanie McMahon Ives
Spanish translation: Cristina de la Torre, in collaboration with Susan Stockdale
Spanish copy editor: Cecilia Molinari
Spanish proofreader: Hercilia Mendizabal

The author and publisher thank Lulu Delacre for her editorial support on the Spanish translation of the poetic text.
The publisher thanks Dr. Kevin de Queiroz, Dr. Dave Johnson, Dr. Rafael Lemaitre, Charyn J. Micheli, Dr. Jon Norenburg, Dr. Ross Robertson, and René Valdés for their guidance regarding Spanish animal names.
The illustrations were created in acrylic on paper.

On the front cover: Spotted Owl
On the back cover: jaguar

Manufactured in September 2016 by RR Donnelley & Sons in China
10 9 8 7 6 5 4 3 2 1
First Edition

Library of Congress Cataloging-in-Publication Data

Names: Stockdale, Susan, author, illustrator. | De la Torre, Cristina, translator. | Stockdale, Susan. Spectacular spots. | Stockdale, Susan. Spectacular spots. Spanish.
Title: Spectacular spots = Magníficas manchas / written and illustrated by = escrito e ilustrado por Susan Stockdale ; translation by = traducción de Cristina de la Torre.
Other titles: Magníficas manchas
Description: First bilingual trade paperback edition. | Atlanta, Georgia : Peachtree Publishers, 2017. | Text in English and Spanish. | Audience: Ages 2-6. | Audience: K to grade 3.
Identifiers: LCCN 2016045584 | ISBN 9781561459780
Subjects: LCSH: Animals—Color—Juvenile literature. | Camouflage (Biology)—Juvenile literature.
Classification: LCC QL767 .S765 2017 | DDC 591.47/2—dc23
LC record available at https://lccn.loc.gov/2016045584

I am deeply grateful to many scientists for their valuable research assistance as I developed the text and illustrations for this book. They include Dr. Kevin de Queiroz, Dr. Carla Dove, Dr. Jerry Harasewych, Dr. Kristofer Helgen, Dr. Robert Hershler, Mr. Gary F. Hevel, Dr. Dave Johnson, Dr. Victor G. Springer, and Dr. Ellen Strong, all with the Smithsonian Institution's National Museum of Natural History, and Dr. Natalia J. Vandenberg of the U.S. Department of Agriculture. I thank them all for their generous and cheerful support in helping me bring *Spectacular Spots* to life.

Agradezco profundamente a varios científicos por su valiosa ayuda en la investigación de este libro mientras desarrollaba el texto y las ilustraciones. Entre ellos se encuentran el señor Gary F. Hevel y los doctores Kevin de Querioz, Carla Dove, Jerry Harasewych, Christopher Helgen, Robert Herschler, Dave Johnson, Victor G. Springer y Ellen Strong, todos del Museo de Historia Natural del Instituto Smithsonian, así como la doctora Natalia J. Vandenberg del Departamento de Agricultura de Estados Unidos. Les quedo muy agradecida a todos por su generosa y animosa ayuda en la creación de *Magníficas manchas*.

Spots on creatures all around,
Manchas en seres vivos por doquier,

way up high

por lo alto

and on the ground.
y por lo bajo.

Spots on snakes

Manchas en culebras

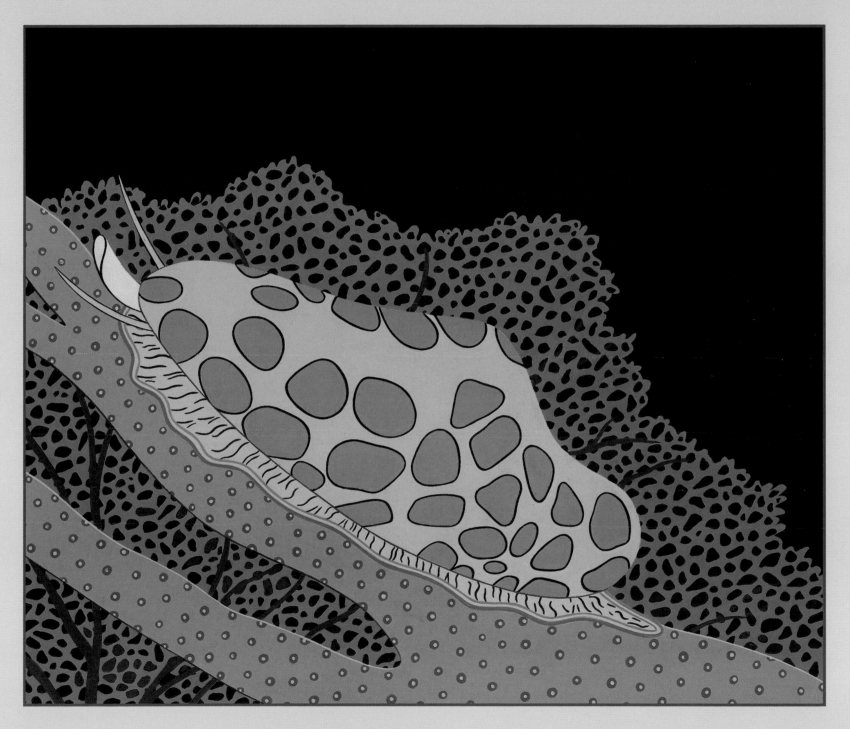

and gliding snails.

y caracoles que se arrastran.

Swimming turtles,
Tortugas nadadoras,

singing quails.
codornices cantarinas.

Crawling crabs

Cangrejos escurridizos

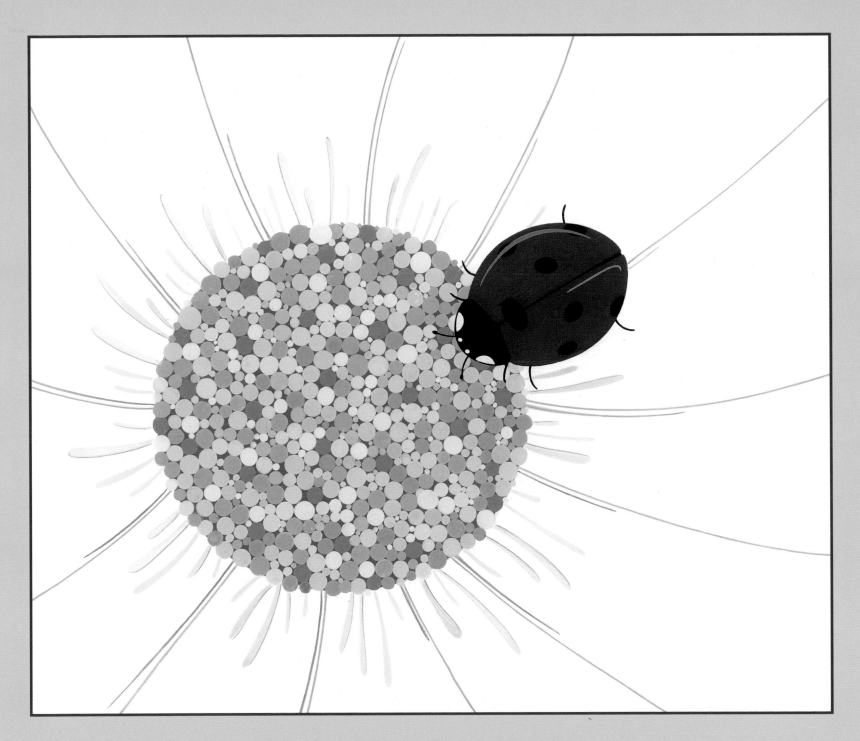

and munching bugs.
y mariquitas que meriendan.

Charging cheetahs,
Guepardos al acecho

creeping slugs.
y babosas sigilosas.

Dashing horses,
Caballos galopantes,

dozing hogs.

cerdos somnolientos.

Scouting fish

Peces exploradores

and clinging frogs.
y ranitas que se adosan.

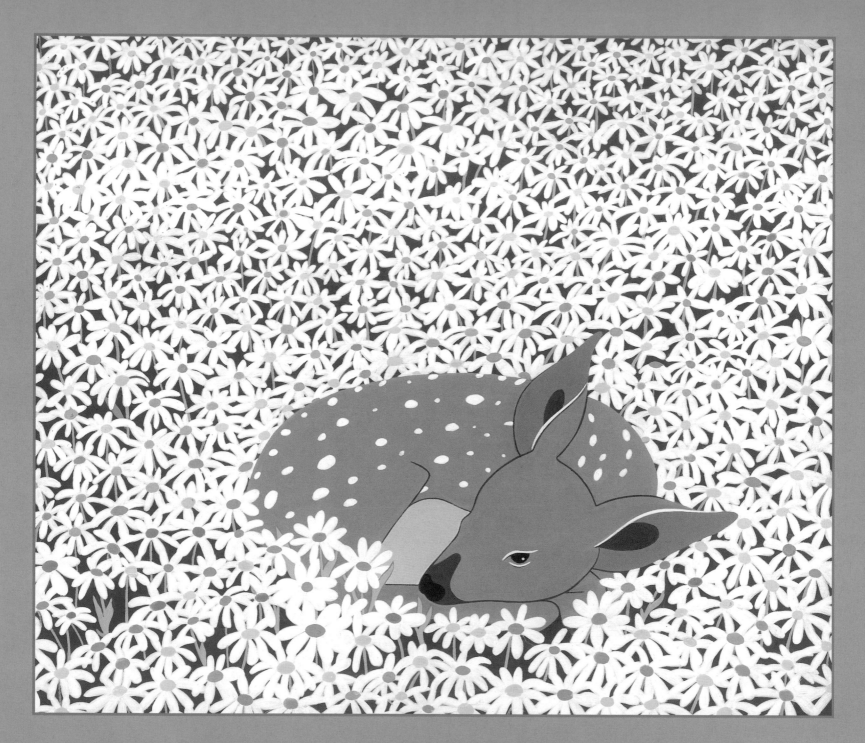

Napping fawn

Cervatillos adormecidos

and strutting fowl.

y gallinas de paseo.

Grazing cattle,

Ganado que pasta,

swooping owl.
búho en calada.

Spots with purpose, spots with flair.

Manchas con motivo, manchas que decoran.

Spotted creatures everywhere!
¡seres vivos con manchas por doquier!

Can you find the animals that belong to these SPOTS?

¿Puedes decir a qué animales pertenecen estas MANCHAS?

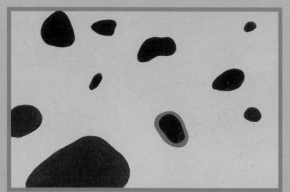

Appaloosa horse / caballo apalusa

jaguar / jaguar

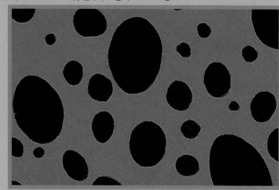

Spotted Owl / Búho moteado

Montezuma Quail / Codorniz de Moctezuma

Dalmatian / dálmata

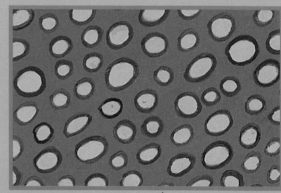

blue poison dart frog / rana flecha azul

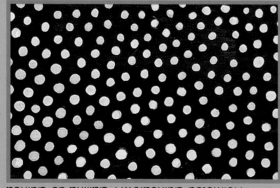

Helmeted Guineafowl / Gallina de Guinea

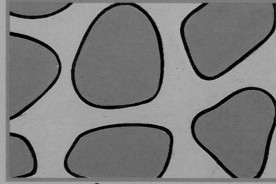

flamingo tongue snail / caracol lengua de flamenco

Buckeye butterfly / Mariposa Junonia coenia

cheetah / guepardo

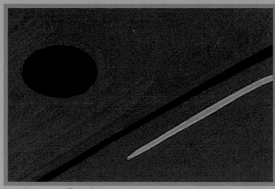

ladybug / mariquita

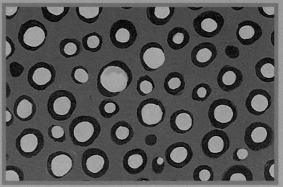

blue boxfish / pez cofre manchado

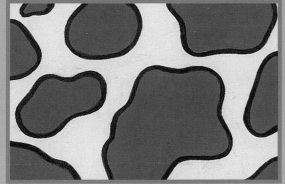

calico crab / cangrejo calico

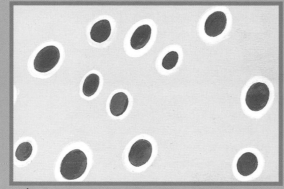

nudibranch / nudibranquio

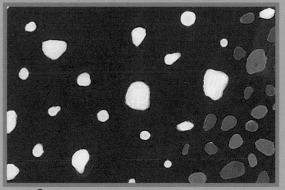

leatherback turtle / tortuga laúd

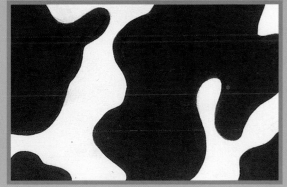

Holstein cow / vaca Holstein

white-tailed deer fawn / cervatillo de cola blanca

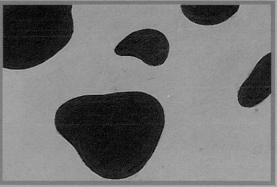

hog / cerdo

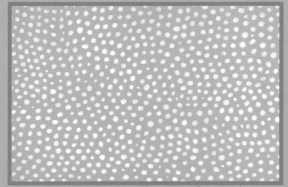

spotted ground squirrel / ardillón punteado

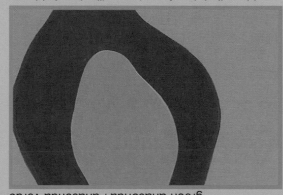

green anaconda / anaconda verde

Turn the book upside down to read the correct answers.

Dale la vuelta al libro y encontrarás las respuestas correctas.

"Eyespots" on a **Buckeye butterfly** mimic the eyes of a larger creature, scaring off predators that might want to eat it. (Caribbean, Mexico and the southernmost parts of the United States; insect)

Las "manchas de ojos" de la **Mariposa Junonia coenia** imitan los ojos de un animal mucho más grande y sirven para ahuyentar a los predadores que puedan querer comérsela. (El Caribe, México y las zonas más al sur de Estados Unidos; insecto)

The **jaguar** and the **spotted ground squirrel** blend in with their surroundings as a result of their spots. (jaguar: Southwestern United States to South America, mammal; spotted ground squirrel: Canada to Mexico; mammal)

El **Jaguar** y la **ardillón punteado** se esconden a simple vista en su entorno gracias a sus manchas. (Jaguar: desde el suroeste de Estados Unidos hasta América del Sur; mamífero. Ardillón punteado: desde Canadá hasta México; mamífero)

Dark green spots on the **green anaconda** help hide it in the leafy jungle. Green anacondas are the heaviest snakes in the world, weighing up to 550 pounds (250 kg). (South America; reptile)

Las manchas verde oscuro ayudan a la **anaconda verde** a desaparecer entre las hojas de la selva. Las anacondas verdes —las serpientes más pesadas del mundo— pueden alcanzar las 550 libras (250 kg). (América del Sur; reptil)

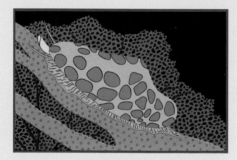

Predators are warned away by the colorfully patterned shell of the **flamingo tongue snail.** It feeds on poisonous sea coral, becoming toxic itself but remaining unharmed. (Tropical waters of the Western Atlantic Ocean including the Caribbean Sea; mollusk)

Los predadores se mantienen alejados del **caracol lengua de flamenco** gracias a las manchas de colores de su concha. Se alimenta de corales venenosos que lo convierten en tóxico sin hacerle daño. (Aguas tropicales del Océano Atlántico occidental, incluyendo el mar Caribe; molusco)

The dappled black shell of the **leatherback turtle** blends well with the dark waters of the open ocean. Leatherbacks are the largest of all living turtles. (All tropical and subtropical oceans, extending into the Arctic Circle; reptile)

El caparazón salpicado de manchas de la **tortuga laúd** la hace casi invisible en las oscuras aguas del mar abierto. Estas tortugas son las más grandes de todas las vivas en la actualidad. (Todos los mares tropicales y subtropicales

The male **Montezuma Quail** sings nine descending notes in a whinnying call to attract a mate. Its patterned feathers help this ground-dwelling bird avoid detection by predators. (Mexico and Southwestern United States; bird)

La **Codorniz de Moctezuma** macho canta nueve notas descendientes que conforman una seductora llamada a las hembras. Sus plumas jaspeadas ayudan a esconder de sus enemigos a este pájaro que vive en el suelo. (México y el suroeste de Estados Unidos; ave)

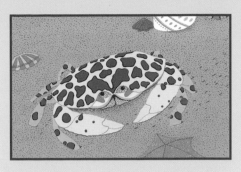

Camouflaged by its patterned shell, the **calico crab** buries itself in the sand. It darts out of its hiding place to seize prey with its sharp claws. (Western Atlantic Ocean from the Chesapeake Bay to the Dominican Republic; crustacean)

La concha moteada le sirve de perfecto camuflaje al **cangrejo calico,** que se entierra bajo la arena y sale disparado de su escondite para atrapar a su presa con sus afiladas pinzas. (Océano Atlántico occidental, desde la bahía de Chesapeake hasta la República Dominicana; crustáceo)

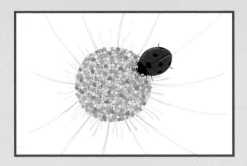

As the **ladybug** feeds on pollen and small insects found on plants, its bright coloring and spots warn enemies away. If disturbed, it emits a bad-smelling fluid. (All parts of the world except Antarctica; insect)

Mientras la **mariquita** se alimenta de polen y de los pequeños insectos que encuentra en las plantas, su brillante colorido y sus manchas mantienen alejados a sus enemigos. Si la molestan, larga un líquido con mal olor. (Todo el mundo menos Antártida; insecto)

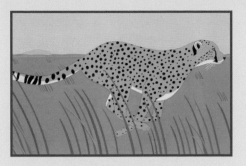

The **cheetah** is camouflaged by its spotted coat as it stalks prey in the tall grasses. It is the fastest land mammal, reaching speeds of up to 75 miles per hour (120 km) in short bursts. (Africa and Asia; mammal)

Las manchas de la piel camuflan al **guepardo** mientras acecha a su presa entre las hierbas altas. Es el mamífero de tierra más veloz, alcanzando hasta las 75 millas (120 km) por hora en carreras cortas a toda velocidad. (África y Asia; mamífero)

Also known as a sea slug, the **nudibranch** often gets its brilliant coloring from the coral, sponges, and anemones it eats. Its colors may warn predators that it is poisonous. (Oceans worldwide; mollusk)

El **nudibranquio,** también conocido como babosa de mar, deriva su brillante colorido del coral, las esponjas y las anémonas de las que se alimenta. Sus colores pueden alertar a sus enemigos de que es venenoso. (Océanos de todo el mundo; molusco)

As it ages, the coat of the **Appaloosa horse** develops a spotted pattern. The coloring and spotting on each horse is unique. Like our fingerprints, no two patterns are exactly alike! (North America; mammal)

A medida que madura, el pelaje del **caballo apalusa** va desarrollando un patrón de manchas. Los colores y la distribución de las manchas son únicos a cada caballo. Al igual que con las huellas digitales de los humanos, ¡no hay dos patrones iguales! (América del Norte; mamífero)

The color and size of spots on the **hog** vary a great deal. Also known as a pig, it is a very intelligent animal with a keen sense of smell. (All continents except Antarctica; mammal)

El color y el tamaño de las manchas del **cerdo** tienen gran variedad. También conocido como puerco, chancho o cochino, es un animal muy inteligente y con un agudo sentido del olfato. (Todos los continentes menos Antártida; mamífero)

Vivid colors on the **blue boxfish** may signal to other ocean animals that it is deadly to eat. The fish needs this protection because it is a very slow swimmer. (Indian and Pacific oceans; fish)

Los vívidos colores del **pez cofre manchado** le indican a otros animales acuáticos que es mortal comérselo. Necesita esta protección ya que nada muy lentamente. (Océanos Pacífico e Índico; pez)

Bright colors and bold spots on the **blue poison dart frog** warn rainforest creatures of its toxic nature. Some poison dart frogs are considered the most poisonous animals in the world. (South America; amphibian)

Los colores brillantes y las marcadas manchas de la **rana flecha azule** anuncian su naturaleza tóxica a otras criaturas de la selva tropical. Algunas variedades son consideradas los animales más venenosos del mundo. (América del Sur; anfibio)

It can be hard for predators to find the **white-tailed deer fawn**; its spotted coat blends in with its surroundings. The spots disappear when the fawn matures. (Canada to South America; mammal)

No es fácil que los predadores encuentren al **cervatillo de cola blanca** ya que su pelaje con manchas hace que se mezcle con el entorno. Las manchas desaparecen cuando el cervatillo crece. (Desde Canadá a América del Sur; mamífero)

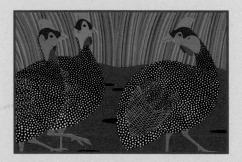

The feathers of the **Helmeted Guineafowl** are often used by people to decorate jewelry, hair ornaments and other products. The male bird attacks other males who try to take his mates by ramming them with the bony "helmet" on his head. Native to Africa but widely introduced elsewhere; bird)

Las plumas con manchas de la **Gallina de Guinea**, se usan a menudo para decorar joyas, adornos para el pelo y otros productos. El macho ataca a otros machos si tratan de quitarle su pareja, embistiéndolos con el "casco" huesudo que tiene en la cabeza. (Oriunda de África pero introducida en otros muchos lugares; ave)

Known for its distinctive black and white markings, the average **Holstein cow** produces about 23,000 pounds (10,400 kg) of milk each year! Many products such as cheese, butter and ice cream are made from milk. (All continents except Antarctica; mammal)

Conocida por sus distintivas marcas en blanco y negro, una **vaca Holstein** promedio ¡normalmente produce hasta 23.000 libras (10,400 kg) de leche al año! Muchos productos como el queso, la mantequilla y el helado se hacen con leche. (Todos los continentes excepto Antártida; mamífero)

The **Spotted Owl** glides silently down to grab small mammals like flying squirrels and woodrats with its talons. Then it kills its prey with its sharp beak, often eating it whole. (United States and Canada; bird)

El **Búho moteado** se desliza silenciosamente hasta el suelo para atrapar con sus garras a pequeños mamíferos como ardillas voladoras o ratas de bosque. Entonces mata a su presa con su afilado pico y a menudo se la come entera. (Estados Unidos y Canadá; ave)

Dalmatian puppies are born completely white and develop spots as they age. A popular companion and pet, the Dalmatian is also used as a rescue dog. (All continents except Antarctica; mammal)

Los cachorros **dálmata** nacen totalmente blancos y a medida que crecen se cubren de manchas. Es una mascota muy popular que también sirve de perro de rescate. (Todos los continentes menos Antártida; mamífero)